To Chris –
for making dreams come true
J. H.

For Helen with love
M. B.

Text copyright ©1998 by Judy Hindley
Illustrations copyright © 1998 by Mike Bostock

First U.S. edition 1998

Library of Congress Cataloging-in-Publication Data

Hindley, Judy.
A song of colors / Judy Hindley ;
illustrated by Mike Bostock.—1st U.S. ed.
p. cm.
Summary: An illustrated collection of poems describing
all sorts of items that represent shades of colors from
red, yellow, and green to pink, brown, and white.

ISBN 0-7636-0320-1
1. Colors—Juvenile poetry.
2. Children's poetry, American.
[1. Color—Poetry. 2. American poetry.]
I. Bostock, Mike, ill. II. Title.
811'.54—dc21   97-6761

10 9 8 7 6 5 4 3 2 1

Printed in Italy

This book was typeset in Weiss
with Monotype Mantinia headings.
The pictures were done in watercolor
and colored ink.

Candlewick Press
2067 Massachusetts Avenue
Cambridge, Massachusetts 02140

A SONG of COLORS

Judy Hindley

illustrated by
Mike Bostock

CANDLEWICK PRESS
CAMBRIDGE, MASSACHUSETTS

BLUE

Blue of distance, blue of sloes,

willow pattern, men in woad;

bright sky blue, electric blue,

delphinium and dolphin blue,

giant-stairs-of-water blue

where the sea steps down

from the shore. . . .

Azure, aqua, indigo,

shadows in the purest snow,

midnight, peacock, royal blue,

true blue, goblin blue;

blue in the glinty flares of ice,

splintery crystal blue of eyes,

hot quick blue of a dragonfly;

blur of blue

that bites through a match

where it burns to a crooked black.

Ice blue, blue of dusk,

robin's egg, forget-me-not;

blue of the bubble of Earth in space,

looking back from the moon.

RED

Shimmering throat
of hummingbird—
a stab, a flash, a splash of it!
Poppies, cherries, roses, bricks,
rubies, blood, and traffic lights.
Studded, clustered berries bright
on wreaths and vines
and autumn hedges;
bunting, flags, and
lipstick kisses;
jeweled glow of rabbit's eyes.
Solemn dark of crimson room,
angry spark of ancient star,
staccato march of palace guard;
length of scarlet path unrolled
for kings
and princesses
and brides.

WHITE

White of paper,
milk, and snow,
ermine trim on royal robes;
white of giant bears and owls,
clouds and daisies, chalk and horn,
a shining castle, sun-bleached bone.
White of gulls that flash and turn
and dip and scatter around the sky.
White of foam. The whites of eyes.
White of ghosts and teeth and stones
and ivory and angel robes;
white of a face when it's ill,
or old, and crinkled as paper.
White that's cold.
White of the smooth inside of an egg.
Froth of white on a birthday cake!
White of moonlight, blue and still,
of seashells, feathers,
pillows,
pearls.

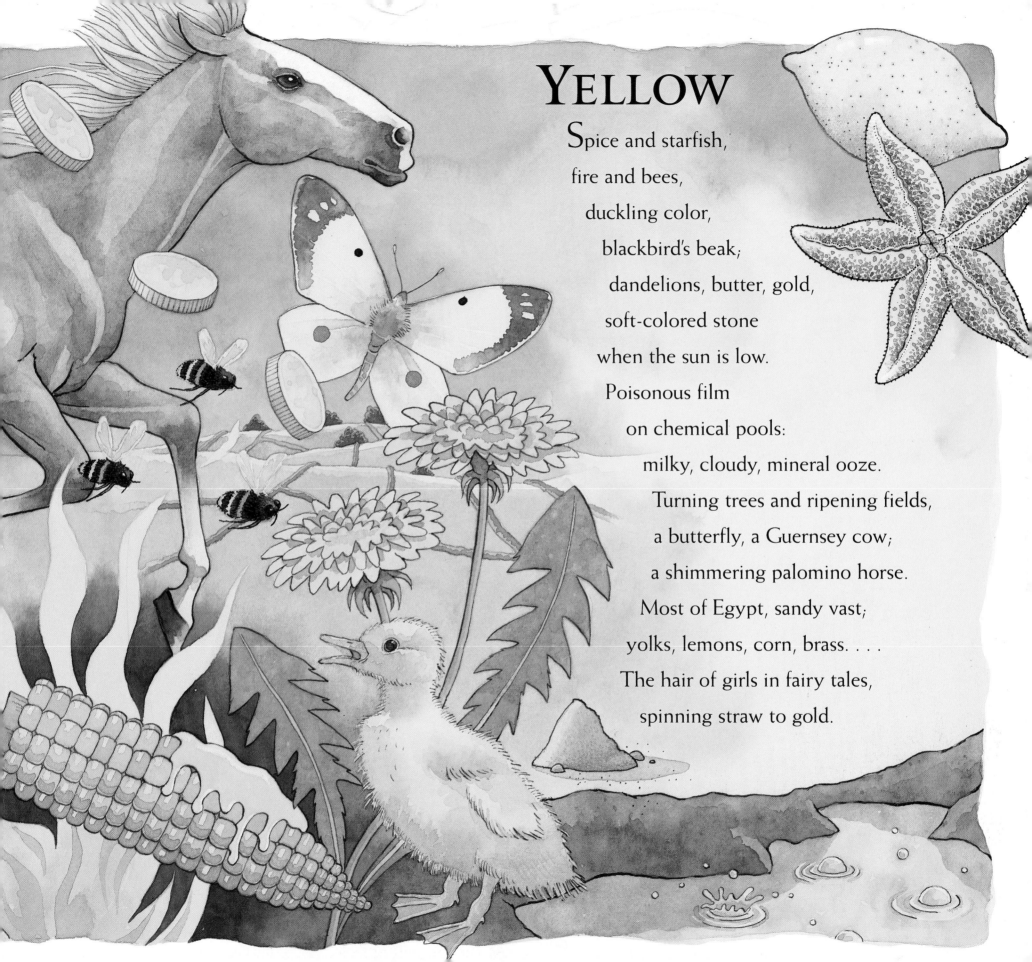

YELLOW

Spice and starfish,

fire and bees,

duckling color,

blackbird's beak;

dandelions, butter, gold,

soft-colored stone

when the sun is low.

Poisonous film

on chemical pools:

milky, cloudy, mineral ooze.

Turning trees and ripening fields,

a butterfly, a Guernsey cow;

a shimmering palomino horse.

Most of Egypt, sandy vast;

yolks, lemons, corn, brass. . . .

The hair of girls in fairy tales,

spinning straw to gold.

PINK

Pink that's shocking,

loud as a shout,

like tropical fish

with fins that furl and flare

outrageously as wings!

Flamingo feathers, coral reefs;

a swollen sun in a sea of cloud

when all the sky is a blaze of pink.

Pink that startles, raw as a prawn;

a sunburned neck, a neon sign;

pink that gleams its tiny lights

in a smear of oil,

in suds, in bubbles.

Pink that's sugary.

Pink that's sweet.

Strawberry ice cream. Fingernails.

Babies' fingers, soles of feet;

the quiet pink,

sometimes,

of dawn—

the huge inside

of a hippo's yawn.

ORANGE

What a comical, cheerful thing it is

in marigolds,

and marmalade,

and gingery, carroty hair—

a toucan's beak,

an occasional cat,

a pumpkin plot,

an apricot.

Then it erupts like Vesuvius,

awesome as tiger fur!

GRAY

Is it dim, or is it bright?

Moss, mouse, rabbit soft,

mushroom, fawn, and fog,

or silvery slate of leafless trees,

pebble beaches,

roofs, and walls?

Does it swim with rainbow lights?

Is it nearly pearly white?

Does it shimmer, does it gleam,

does it glisten, does it glint?

Quartz, opal, pewter, smoke.

A spoon,

a knife,

a rainy dawn.

BROWN

Umber,

amber,

ocher, tan;

honey gold brick

of a mud-built town;

topaz and mahogany;

sienna, sepia, and sand.

Milky chocolate, dun, and snuff;

cobnuts bursting from their pelts;

chestnut, sorrel, roan, and bay;

toffee, coffee, butterscotch.

BLACK

Black of licorice, black of print,
black of charcoal, black of soot;
twisted black of a candlewick.
Panther black. Black of a crow.
Black of the sky
on a moonless midnight
(polished and bedecked with stars).
Black of the dark
in caves and furrows,
pits and rifts and clefts and holes.
Bat and ant and beetle black.
Fresh-laid tarmac, soft and hot.
Highways glistening with rain.
Pitch. Tar.
Iron. Ink.
Jet. Coal. Angus bull.
Black of the loam beneath the gold
where the plow cuts through
the stubble corn—
ebony rooster on a roof,
with a scarlet comb, in the snow.

GREEN

Apple green
and acid green
and olive green
and pea.
Leafy,
grassy,
emerald:
wave, leaf, sea.
Tiny, curly lichen;
moss green,
lawn.
Jade, lime,
bottle green.
Lizard in a weedy pond.

PURPLE

The dark of shadows next to green,

arabesques in a weedy stream;

glossy as eggplant is, or plum;

dim of the clefts

in the twists of a tree;

or scars of mud

on a low green hill

bitten with burrows

of rabbits or moles.

The pale gray glimmering mist of it

in the blur of hundreds

of leafless twigs

where catkins hang their gold.

Mauve, lilac, amethyst;

crocuses, orchids, irises;

maroon, magenta, fuchsia, grape.

The hush of velvet robes.

MANY-COLORED

Many colors, any colors,
splattering in stars:
rocket-bursting multiple explosions
in the dark.
Gleaming buttons in a jar,
glistening like sweets.
Polka dots and sugar drops,
strips and stripes and beads,
and palettes, and kaleidoscopes,
and Joseph's many-colored coat!
Multicolored ribbons streaming
all around a pole,
misty, airy bands of color melting in a bow.
Paisley-pattern butterfly,
peacock-feather shawl,
prisms casting crystal fires
that dance along a wall. . . .

Swirling from the blackness,
whirling into white,
spinning on a color wheel—
dissolving
into light.